Career Awareness Among Post Graduate Agriculture Students

Mahesh Dutt

Copyright © [2023]

Title: Career Awareness Among Postgraduate Agriculture Students

Author Mahesh Dutt

All rights reserved. No part of this publication may be reproduced, stored in a retrieval system, or transmitted in any form or by any means, electronic, mechanical, photocopying, recording, or otherwise, without the prior written permission of the publisher or author, except in the case of brief quotations embodied in critical reviews and certain other noncommercial uses permitted by copyright law.

This book was printed and published by in [2023]

ISBN:

CONTENTS

Sr. No.	CHAPTERS	Page No.
I	INTRODUCTION	1-11
II	REVIEW OF LITERATURE	12-25
III	RESEARCH METHODOLOGY	26-37
IV	RESULTS AND DISCUSSION	38-63
V	CONCEPTUAL FRAME WORK	64-68
VI	SUMMARY AND CONCLUSION	69-73

LIST OF TABLES

Table No.	Description	Page No.
3.1.1	Information about the district (census- 2011)	25
3.1.4	Location and situation of other institution	27
3.2	Total selected respondents from the sample college of agriculture department	28
3.3	Selection of variables and their empirical measurement	28
5.1.1	Distribution of respondents according to age	37
5.1.2	Distribution of respondents according to their educational level	38
5.1.3	Distribution of respondents according to caste	38
5.1.4	Distribution of respondents according to marital status	39
5.1.5	Distribution of respondents according to family type	40
5.1.6	Distribution of respondents according to family size	40
5.1.7	Distribution of respondents according to family occupation	41
5.1.8	Distribution of respondents according to family income (Rs.)	42
5.1.9	Distribution of respondents according to housing pattern	43
5.1.10	Distribution of respondents according to land holding	43
5.1.11	Distribution of respondents according to communication media possession	44

5.1.12	Distribution of respondents according to degree of agreement / disagreement statement of economic motivation.	45
5.1.13	Distribution of respondents according to economic motivation	47
5.1.14	Distribution of respondents according to degree of agreement/ disagreement statement of achievement motivation	48
5.1.15	Distribution of respondents according to achievement motivation	49
5.2.1	Distribution of respondents according to Degree of consciousness about career opportunities	49
5.3.1	Distribution of respondents according to love motivates sources	51
5.3.2	Distribution of respondents according to knowledge motivates sources	52
5.3.3	Distribution of respondents according to compassion motivates sources	53
5.3.4	Distribution of respondents according to economic motivates sources	54
5.4.1	Distribution of respondents according to career preferences	56
5.5.1	Degree of seriousness of constraints	57
5.6	Suggestion measures to overcome the constraints in career preference of agriculture students	58

Chapter-I

INTRODUCTION

In the age of rapid global development, exchange of information, sharing of views, ideas, experience and cooperation are essential for mutual benefits of the participating countries. SAARC was born in 1985 with the above objectives and purposes. Among the SAARC countries, there are many things common in nature, origin, use, stages in development which could be shared and utilized for the progress and welfare of general mass. Historically a strong bondage exists among the peoples of SAARC countries in the way of expressing common values, thinking, reciprocating ideas and showing respects. The peoples in the SAARC countries are living in a small global village where an effective common platform is in operation to make mutual exchange of many things.

The history of agricultural education in India can be traced back to medieval period when study of agriculture was included in the curricula of Nalanda and Takshashila Universities as an important subject. However, formalized courses in agricultural education began only at the beginning of 20th century when six agricultural colleges were established at Kanpur, Lyalpur (now Pakistan), Coimbatore, Nagpur, Pune and Sabour in 1905-06. After independence in 1974,the government of India planning process. To ensure orderly growth, the ICAR took lead and drafted a model act, and encouraged the setting of exclusive State Agricultural Universities (SAUs) for research and education support. The first Agriculturaluniversities in the country

INTRODUCTION

was set in 1960 at Pantnagar (now in Uttarakhand State). In 1978-79, 21 SAUs were established which at present has gone up 63, Five Deemed Agriculture University and Three Central Universities (CUs). Sixty six year ago, **pt. Jawahar Lal Nehru,** the first prime minister of India, said **'Everything else can wait but not agriculture'** which holds true even today, agriculture belonging a driver of country' economic growth .one of the prime focuses of the nation is to ensure food and nutritional security for its burgeoning population.

Agriculture is a booming industry with a wide variety of job to choose from across the globe. In severaljob sectors, those in the agricultural business work to cultivate experiment and market food products. The different industry incorporates many different of skills and employs people with a wide variety of agriculture interests, which shows that there is a job for everyone in agriculture.

Career describes an individual's journey through learning work and other aspects of life. A career is often composed of the jobs held and work accomplished over a long period of time, rather than just referring to one position is known as career. Career choice refers to the intention to enter anoccupation. Career selection is one of many important choice's students will make in determining plans. This decision will impart them throughout their lives. Career awareness means gaining knowledge of career paths and job opportunities and the skills and qualifications necessary to be successful in these positions. According to the Ministry of labor & employment, Govt. of India, out of all university graduates only a meager 13% are employable.

Agriculture is a potential employment generation sector in India. About 54.6% of the population depends on it for their revenue.

INTRODUCTION

Agriculture being a primary sector dealing with raw material production, it supports the other sectors like manufacturing sector and service sector. Many stakeholders like starting from farmers, input dealers, traders, processing companies, government agencies, private firms, non-governmental Organizations (NGOs) etc. are striving for the sustainable development of agriculture. With the declining population contribution to farming and shrinking resources there is a serious threat to food and nutritional security to the Nation. Hence, a technically sound manpower is needed to be built to support the existing farming community and also to take up farming. Agricultural educations is the route map to attain a quality manpower trained with the agricultural practices In India, agricultural education has seen several stages growth over thousands years. However, no formal education system was reported until the 19th century in agriculture. Later, the need for formal agricultural research and education system was realized from the 20th century and several initiatives have commenced. Agricultural education and extension have been geared to harness the modern science and technology for higher productivity and production Unknown (2014).

Agricultural careers may be divided into various categories. Such as: Agribusiness management, Natural resources and communications, Agricultural and research, Agriculture production, Building construction management, Resource development and management, Park and packing, Food science, Horticulture, Forestry and Fisheries / Wildlife.Different other posts are Assistant professor, Assistant scientists, District extension specialist, Assistant plant pathology, Assistant bacteriologist, Assistant botanist, Assistant research

INTRODUCTION

scientist, Assistant breeder, junior pedologist, Subject matter specialist.

The agriculture students today are better scientifically equipped to deal with the administrative matters and development programmers but satirically most of the agriculture students today are not the employed for which they are specially educated. The career opportunities for the employment of agriculture students are the immense and could be in the field such as State Department of Agriculture, Private Sectors, Banks, Agriculture field officer, Post-harvest Technology, Privatization if extension for self- employment etc.

The modern era agriculture science education has become more complex and specialized which offers many career opportunities for agricultural students. Agriculture science students have some plans to purpose a specific career after getting their degree. They do aspire for a remunerative job.Agriculture student has various career avenues on the basis of his/her own liking and disliking after completing under graduation/Post-graduation and Doctorate studies.

It is one of the largest national networks of AES in the world, comprising 63 State Agricultural Universities (SAUs), 4 Deemed-to be- universities, 3 Central Agricultural University and four Central Scientific way of crop protection Universities having agriculture faculty.ICAR works in a partnership mode with SAUs and has contributed significantly in developing first rate human resource by way of co-coordinating, supporting and guiding various aspects of higher agricultural education. It provides funds for development and strengthening facilities in vital areas, training to faculty and scholarships/fellowships to the students for quality assurance. To reduce the inbreeding in agricultural education, students are being encouraged to other states for pursuing their higher studies by providing the National Talent Scholarship, Junior Research Fellowships and SRF (PGS).*(DARE ANNUAL REPORT 2012-13)*

The Gross Enrolment Ratio for Agricultural Education, out of the total eligible Population in the country is only 0.03% and against the total eligible rural population, it is 0.04% which is quite low. Low access of agricultural education to rural students, non-contemporary course curricula and delivery methods, inadequate state funding, unplanned proliferation of SAUs and colleges, regional Imbalances in agricultural education facilities, lecture methods still dominating the teaching, lack of brand value for most of SAUs, complete disconnect between the Requirements of industry and the education being imparted, poor quality education Imparted in 158 private colleges and 41 colleges under 15 general universities Admitting about 10,000 students, gender inequality, mismatch of infrastructure for quality education, research & extension, extensive inbreeding in faculty recruitment, poor faculty strength, poor governance, lack of environment for nurturing and retaining talent, lack of faculty – competence in cutting edge technologies low priority to agricultural education as career option & declining quality of students admitted, growing unemployment (43%graduates,25% post-graduates), shifting employment opportunities from public to private sector.

Many stakeholders like starting from farmers, input dealers, traders, processing companies, government agencies, private firms, non–governmental Organizations (NGOs) etc. are striving for the sustainable development of agriculture. With the declining population contribution to farming and shrinking resources there is a serious threat to food and nutritional security to the Nation. Hence, a technically sound manpower is needed to be built to support the existing farming community and to take up farming. Agricultural educations are the route map to attain a quality manpower trained with the agricultural practices in India, agricultural education has seen several stages growth over thousand years. However, no formal education system was reported until the 19th century in agriculture. Late on, the need for formal agricultural research and education system was realized from the 20th century and several initiatives have commenced. Agricultural education and extension have been geared to harness the modern science and technology for higher productivity and production unanimous (2014).

Universities exclusively imparting agricultural education are less than 10% of all the universities in India. Similarly, colleges exclusively imparting agricultural education are less than 1% of all colleges. And the student enrolment in such colleges is close to 0.5% of all student enrolment in higher education. Thus, agricultural education in India is not for producing professional farmers. There are close to 14 crores agricultural land-holdings in the country. So, at least that many households can be called farming households. Even if we consider one child from each household to get agricultural education, it will take centuries of agricultural education at the current enrolment rate. If we want professional farmers, we need to strengthen the agricultural education infrastructure substantially. Therefore, the statement viz. 'agricultural graduates do not practice agriculture' is not well-founded. Agricultural education is for producing professionals who can intervene in the farming process through various employments (research and development, manufacturing of inputs, marketing of inputs, catalysts for adoption). By creating more and better opportunities in the above mentioned main agricultural sectors, it is possible to persuade agricultural graduates from opting for other fields like civil services and banking. **(Source: AISHE 2015-16 http://aishe.nic.in)**

Adding professionalism to agriculture and allied sciences is necessary. It is essential that agricultural graduates come up with start-up ventures in a big way. This requires providing special packages for graduates volunteering to practice agriculture with modern technology. Special concessions and subsidies to purchase farm machineries and equipment's for setting up of custom hiring centers are necessary to act as service providers, facilitators or mediators between farmers and industry.

Future Prospect of Agricultural graduates has a major role and contribution in the nation building process of various aspects including food production and food safety, elimination of hunger and poverty, continue better economic growth through establishment of new agro-based industries. Considering the national development process, the future prospect of agricultural graduates is keenly bright in comparison to any other single professions. Agricultural graduates can contribute and play a vital role in many organizations.

Further, there is need for agricultural graduates having knowledge, skill, ability and also entrepreneurship to provide a class of village-based services such as diagnostic laboratories, advisories on new innovations, markets and avenues of development assistance for corporate and contract farming. Industry and universities partnership are essential. If industries are to obtain well-trained

INTRODUCTION

agricultural professionals in cutting edge technologies for international competitiveness.

The following career opportunities exist for those who have completed a B.Sc. (Ag.) like as Agricultural policy advisor, Banking and Finance analyst, Agricultural marketing, product manager, Agribusiness manager, Market and Policy analyst, Agricultural training

officer, Subject matter specialist and Agricultural extension officer. Whatever your career interest lies on the production or consumer side or somewhere in between, a Bachelor of science degree in Agriculture with an emphasis in sustainable agriculture will provide you with the skills and knowledge to incorporate economic viability, environmental stewardship, and social responsibilities in food and farming systems. Your tailored degree program will prepare you for many career opportunities. Some careers you might consider include:

- **Production**: Operate your own farm and produce high quality and sustainable agricultural products for private companies local, national or international markets.
- **Sales and Marketing:** Work for retailers, wholesalers, cooperatives or direct marketing initiatives that recognize the growing consumer demand for eco-sustainable raised products. Potential employers include whole foods, and by products.
- **Government:** A variety of local, state and national agencies provide various career opportunities in the areas of conservation, data and policy analysis, rural and international

development. The potential employers include State Cooperative Extension and agencies within the U.S. Department of Agriculture.

- **Non-Government Organizations:** it is a part of an organizations that work based on agricultural and environmental issues, community and economic development or development of eco-sustainable food systems. The potential employers include local, national and international non-profits, grassroots farmer and consumer organizations and food initiatives.
- **Research/Internship Opportunities:** Agricultural students are required to complete a three- credit -hour internship or international experiences in sustainable agriculture. You will find many career opportunities are available for internship and research that reflect the variety of innovative food and farming systems and your own interests. Keeping in view all the above facts into consideration, the present study was undertaken with following objectives:

1. To study the profile of the respondents.
2. To study the consciousness of the respondents about career opportunities.
3. To study the motivational sources for career opportunities.
4. To study preference of the respondents about career opportunities.
5. To analyses the constraints regarding conscious job opportunities and fulfilling preferences and suggestions to overcome the constraints there of.

INTRODUCTION

Important/justification of this study:

1. The present study is an attempt to explore the valuable preference for career which is played by agricultural students in different sector.
2. This study would be helpful for raising of socio-economic status of agricultural students.
3. This study would help to identifying the trends of jobs liking and disliking of the students of agriculture degree in respect of career.
4. This study also will be helpful for career planners and extension workers in formulation of strategies for increasing the involvement of agricultural students for better career job opportunities options.

Limitations:

1. This research was conduct in only in Kanpur and Ajodhya district of Utter Pradesh.
2. The time and resource at the disposal of investigator are also important limiting factor.
3. The finding is based on the study conducted only one agriculture college of two Agriculture Universities situated in district of Kanpur and Ayodhya of U.P. therefore, the results cannot be used for generalization.
4. The study was restricted few to few variables, due to limited time and resources.
5. The present study is limited for job preference of agricultural students, but there is also possibility of including other variables to be stored.

INTRODUCTION

6. The conclusion is based on the data provided by the respondents; therefore, the validity and reliability depend on the how honestly, they provided the information.

Chapter-II

REVIEW OF LITERATURE

Review of literature is a very important step for any scientific research, as it is helps in generalization results. It provides a theoretical framework for the proposed study. An attempt has been made to review the literature, which is meaningful, and had direct relevance to this study. The available researches have been presented under the following sub heads:

1. Profile of the respondents.
2. Consciousness of the respondents about career opportunities.
3. Motivational sources for career opportunities.
4. Preference of the respondents about career opportunities.
5. Constraints regarding conscious job opportunities and fulfilling preferences and suggestions to overcome the constraints there of.

1. Studies on socio- economic Profile of the respondents:

Ferry (2006) Observed that schooling is one of the cultural and socio-economic factors that affect the choice of career of the youths.

Akinsorotan *et al.* (2007) revealed that 43.9% of the respondents were males and 56.1 % were female it also shown that most of the respondents (93.9%) were 18 years and above. It was discovered that majority of respondent's parent (90.8% father and 88.8% mothers) occupation were non farming occupation while only a few (9.3% of the fathers and 11.2% mothers) were involved in farming occupation.

REVIEW OF LITERATURE

Onuekwusi and Ijeoma(2008) stated that the majority of the students were in the group of 18-20 years, Majority, 51% of the students were female and 49% were male. The respondent's background was rural (farming) and most of student's parent engaged more in farming. About 74% were influenced by their parents, on career decision, 28% of respondents were to pursue a non-agricultural related university degree,30% of respondents were having negative attitude towards farming/agriculture and 70% were having positive attitude towards farming/agriculture.

Carpenter (2009)reported that specifically, it described the academic performance of graduating agriculture students, identified the personal, socio- economic and educational factors that relate to academic performance and determined the extent to which these factors influenced academic performance.

Gathiagia(2011)reported that over 71 per cent of the career choice decision made by the students were based on their academic abilities.

Gude(2017)stated that majority (84.16%) of the students were good in their academic achievements, while (13.32%) were excellent in their academic achievement and very few (2.5%) illustrated average performance in their academic achievement.

Ashwini barge (2018)noticed that more than half (60.00%) of the respondents were in first class category, followed by 20.83 per cent, 19.16 per cent of them in distinction and second-class category, respectively.

REVIEW OF LITERATURE

2. Consciousness of the respondents about career opportunities

Sukhdev *et at.*(1999)Stated that students of the B.Sc. colleges located in rural, semi-urban and urban areas (India), examined the career awareness of the students. Variables such as family size, parental income and education were studied. None of the students studying in government college (either from urban/semi-urban or rural areas) had high levels of career awareness, whereas 54% of students studying in public schools had higher levels of career awareness.

Rose (2001) Reported that future harvest promotes the importance of international agricultural research by establishing links between the 5 pillars through international studies and another research, and communicating them through an innovative outreach programme. The roles of agricultural ambassadors that speak out on agricultural issues, commissioned studies, and the media in creating awareness of the importance of agricultural research is considered. It is concluded that Future Harvest is creating opportunities to support international agricultural research.

Ross (2001) Stated that when starting these courses, postgraduate students expect their program to be mostly similar to their undergraduate experience but different in scope. In a study of first postgraduate students at the University of Melbourne, most students pursued postgraduate study to advance their careers and acquire new knowledge within their subject area.

Bowen (2003) The information about courses and careers can be gathered form personal and media sources. A study of public relation students suggested that impersonal mass media impressions influenced coerces and career expectation. While some portrayals of public relations as a

REVIEW OF LITERATURE

glamorous career persuade students select public relation, argues that journalist's negative portrayals of the practiced of public relation influenced other students' perceptions of careers in the discipline.

Roy, J.J. (2005) Stated that careers awareness, investigations of aquaculture and marine trade, enhancement of leadership techniques and the practical application of problem-solving strategies thought application learned skills in the field.

Ramirez *et al.*(2009)Reported that career opportunities to main actors and authorise at the faculty like the dean, college directors, department' coordinators, teachers and students in order to design the narrative structure of the short movie. Recordings were made at different facilities of Los Andes University, Merida, Barinas and Táchira states.

Barrick *et al.*(2011)Stated that most students were generally satisfied with advice received and resources available. Differences exist between Master iof Science and doctoral students in terms of productivity, which is not unexpected given the goals of the separate programs and the time committed to complete the degree. More opportunities to gain teaching experience would be helpful for student's which anticipants an academic career.

Herren *et al.*(2011)Revealed that assess the relative importance of available sources of information during recruiting, institutional characteristics (e.g placement rate and degree program requirements) and personal influences on the timing of a student's decision to attend CASNR at OSU. Nearly 93% of participants agreed the recruiting materials were satisfactory in providing enough information to make a college choice. Survey respondents indicated campus visit were most useful of information.

REVIEW OF LITERATURE

Govindagowda*et al.*(2012)reported that, joining at agriculture and its related degree programme is boon to the students, this was agreed by 50% of students. As students of agriculture are exposed to wide range of subjects this was agreed and strongly agreed by 44% and 41% of students respectively. Three fourth of the students agreed that the practical classes, village visits, study tours were conducted to provide an opportunity to students to become closer to the real-life situation. Teacher in the college used to keep the students informed about the update knowledge of the subjects and this was agreed by nearly 50% of the students.

Settle *et al.*(2012)reported that non-agriculture students experienced increases in self-efficiency for agricultural communications tasks, self-efficacy toward overcoming obstacles for perusing a degree in agricultural communications and interest in agricultural communications careers. Agricultural student was statistically significant for both self-efficacy constructs but not for career interest.

James and Denis (2015)revealed that the 57.4 per cent of the respondents agreed that agriculture is a prestigious career to pursue while 42.6 per cent either disagreed of said they did not know.

Gude(2017) similarly agricultural education was most preferred areas of career among the female students followed by agricultural research, agricultural banking, self-employment/ agri-business, service in extension, agro industry/ private job, farming, NGOs and agricultural journalism respectively.

3.Motivational sources for career opportunities:

Furnham & zacherl (1986)looked at the relationship between personality and job satisfaction in a group of computer specialists. They found that, overall, extraversion (and lie scales) were modestly positively correlated with job satisfaction, while psychoticism and neuroticism were negatively correlated with all seven specifics, and the overall combined, job satisfaction scores.

Staw and Ross (1985) reported that worker attitudes (motivation and satisfaction) are as much function of stable personality traits as organizational conditions. "job attitudes may reflect a biological based trait that predisposes individuals to see positive or negative content in their lives."

Paskova(1989) found that students at agricultural universities in Czechoslovakia are studies particular interest in a subject, the desire for education and need to fulfil personal capabilities are the most commonly cited reasons. Method are discussed whereby the selection procedure can determine those students with little real enthusiasm for study or those with motives prestige and higher income earning capacity.

Barkley *et al.* (1999) founded that salaries were significantly influenced by major field, advanced degrees, job location, gender and family variables, motivation for accepting a job and job mobility. Salary structures were estimated separately male and female alumni.

Scarborough and Miller (2003) reported that communal needs could differ from one society to the other as a need that is not important in one society could be important for another. Therefore, it is apparent that people's life satisfaction (motivation) can be change from one culture to other.

Hughes and Desbrow(2005) found that most common motivation for becoming a dietician was a long – term primary interest in nutrition, health and helping people inspired by previous experience with other dieticians, family or personal illnesses and significant others such as mother and teachers. Approximately 30% of applicants reported being motivated by personal experiences (self or friends). High – level communication and organizational skills and nutrition knowledge were the common competency expectations of dieticians among potential students. Most reported working clinically, running a private practice (particularly in sports nutrition) or in mixed practice settings with autonomy and practice diversity as long -term career aspirations.

Siemens (2005) reported that administrators must motivate themselves in order to achieve high performance in addition to motivating their employees.

Vazquez *et al.* (2009) suggest that the transit through university doesn't foster in an appropriate way the entrepreneurial potential of students, they showing low intentions to start a business as professional career and negative attitudes towards entrepreneurial behaviours. Paradoxically, results also show that first-year students feel relative confident in their personal skills for entrepreneurship, and knowledge and abilities acquired at the university foster students' self-efficacy even more.

Litzenberg, K.K. (2010) observed that some characteristics about the students, they have experiencing a difficult career selection process since their parents are expecting them to select a career path and they are prone to procrastination.

Herren *et al.* (2011) reported that the most useful source of information, career opportunities after graduation and academic reputation were the two most influential institutional characteristics influencing college choice, while parents or graduations were the people providing the strongest influence during the decisions process.

Kowalski (2011) founded that the variable of the number of students affects the internal motivation sources of the teachers. As the number of students decreased, the points obtained by the teachers from the intrinsic motivation scale increase. It is thought that student academic success could increase when there are a decreased number of students in schools/classes. Therefore, as students' successes 'increase, teachers may experience progress and satisfaction more often: in other words, it can increase their intrinsic motivation.

Govindagowda*et al.*(2012) found that 62% students, as they get opportunity to learn by doing as it is known that "practice makes perfect". Counselling is conducted in every semester, 46% of responds strongly agrees and 42% were agreeing to this statement. More than 70% of students were comfortable in understanding the courses.42% agreed that hostile environment was conducive for their study and career at agriculture college.

Lussier & Achua (2015) stated that teaching is a versatile professional field that in corporates social, psychological an economic characteristic in different dimensions. The concept of motivation as a psychological dimension plays and important role for the teachers, students and administrators in the field of education, as in all other field. Motivation is defined as an internal desire for the satisfaction of needs.

Nishitha and Lakshminarayan (2015)conducted that most of the respondents (53.00%) had aspired to increase the land holding by 1-5 acres, while 60.00 pec cent and 80.00 per cent of the respondents aspired to purchase basic agricultural implements and increase the crops productions in next years, respectively.

REVIEW OF LITERATURE

Nataraju*et al.*(2017)concluded that size of land holding was significantly associated with the aspiration and participation of respondents in agriculture.

Ali (2018)study of educational aspiration and academic achievement of senior secondary school students in relation to gender and area observed that educational aspirations have positive and contributory effect on the academic achievement of students.

4. Preference of the respondents about career opportunities

Ziejewski T. (1991)stated that issues, findings are presented on the motivation, aspirations and attitudes of final year students, then on graduate's career paths, their life course, and means of looking for employment. The preparation of graduates for professional posts.

Scofied(1994)reported that students are giving considerable through their occupational choice. Students are looking for job security. He further reported that students also believe that agriculture is vital to the future success of the American economy. He also stated that social status is viewed as important when selected earlier. Nine out of ten students indicated that parents looked favourable upon their career choice.

Brown & Hackett (1996) said that career choice is affected by beliefs that the individual develops and refines through four main sources: a) the personal performance accomplishments, b) vicarious learning, c) social persuasion, d) physiological states and reactions.

Cubric(1997) reported that the majority of students regard the 'instrumental' aspect of learning Italian (i.e., enabling them to use their knowledge in their future profession) as most important, followed by the 'educational' aspect, 'communication' aspect and

REVIEW OF LITERATURE

'cultural' aspect. Written form of the language is not considered important. It is concluded that these results should be taken into consideration by language teachers in their planning of language courses and curricula.

Jones and Larke(2001) suggested that when the respondents enrolled in their first agriculture related course did not affect the probability that they would select ab agriculture related career most of the graduates in this study (62%) did not enroll in their first agriculture related class until college. They further reported that parents' level of education did not pay a role in the respondents choosing an agricultural related career. A low association existed between parents' level of education and employment in agriculture. Also, the difference between respondents employed in an agriculture-related career were not found to be a factor when considering parents level of education.

Ross (2001) reported that when starting these courses, postgraduate students expect their program to be mostly similar to their undergraduate experience but different in scope. In a study of first year postgraduate students at the University of Melbourne most students pursued postgraduate study to advance their careers and acquire new knowledge within subject area.

Kumar and Sujan(2003) concluded that the attitude of the students towards agricultural education swigged between favourable and highly favourable. majority of them had medium level of entrepreneurial orientation. The order of preference for career choice was hob in stare department of agricultural, banks, agricultural universities, private sector, self- employment, NGO and farming as most preferred to least preferred.

Bowen (2003) information about courses and careers can be gathered from personal and media sources. A study of public relationship students

REVIEW OF LITERATURE

suggested that impersonal mass media impressions influenced course and career expectations. While some portrayals of public relations, argues that journalists' negative portrayal of the practiced of public relations influenced of the students' perceptions of careers in the discipline.

AlMiskry*et al.***(2009)**reported that there was a significant difference of realistic career interest pattern between male and female students.

Gathigia(2011) stated that over 71% of career choices decisions made by students were based on their academic abilities, family influence and peer pressure.

Edwards and Migunde(2011) reported that students' career choices are influenced by numerous factors including outcome expectancies, individual variant such as gender, personal interests, learning experiences, environmental factors and personal contacts. Outcome expectancies were the most influential factors in students' career choices however gender and the environment play a very minimal role when it comes to career choice. There are variations in the level of influence each factor has on students' career choices by gender. Family members are more influential in students' career choices as compared to other persons. As students interact with their peers, their advice is less important as compared to family members, teachers and career counsellors.

Govindagowda*et al.* **(2012)** stated that, joining at agriculture and its related degree programme is boon to the students, this was agreed by 50 percent of the students. As students of agriculture are exposed to wide range of subjects this was agreed and strongly agreed by 44 % and 41 % of student's respectively. Three fourth of the students agreed that the practical classes, village visits, study tours were conducted to provide an opportunity to students to become closer to their real-life situation.

Teachers in the college used to keep the students informed about the update knowledge of the subjects and this was agreed by nearly 50 % of the students.

Mondal (2014) perception of agriculture students towards self-employment revealed that majority (50.00%) of the respondents used newspapers as sources of job placement followed by journal (24.28%) and only 5.72 per cent of the respondents used radio as a mass media sources.

Pandey et al. (2017) conducted a study entitled usage of ICAR e-learning portal among students of north east India: a pilot study among students of north east India and observed that around 85 per cent of the respondents said that access to internet improves leaning and the contents were found significant by around 80 per cent of the respondents.

5. Constraints regarding conscious job opportunities and fulfilling preferences and suggestions to overcome the constraints there of.

George (1990) indicated that 59% the students plan to seek initial positions in the food production area and 22% as management trainees. By the fifth year after graduation over 38% wish to be in management and 38% in the food production area. Those enrolled in apprenticeship programmes indicated somewhat greater interest in ownership than those not enrolled in them. Many of the students indicated an interest in hotel/motel management.

Johnson (1996) found that on balance, respondents overwhelmingly believed that expected benefits outweigh possible problems. 80% of respondents reported a generally supportive attitude from their administration, but 75% indicated that the department itself needs to provide leadership in the search for new international linkages.

REVIEW OF LITERATURE

Countryman (2005) observed that the hotel industry pays better than the club industry; however, differences in these two segments may explain some of the variation in compensation. From the analysis, it is apparent that being a controller is a viable career path for individuals interested in working in the hospitality.

Bryant (2006) stated that demonstrate the centrality in the dominant students discourses of masculinities and femininities and how these shape career pathways for women intending to enter occupations in agriculture. Within the discourses it is apparent how embodied power is acted upon and where it is resisted in constituting emerging constructions of occupations that are gendered and sexualized.

Akinsorotal*et at.* (2007) suggested that expansion of college agricultural programme of Oyo State activities, provision of effective agricultural instructors, and release capital support by the government and making college agricultural programme of Oyo State activities more interesting through provision of incentive.

Vazquez *et al.* (2009) point out the need of incorporating entrepreneurship training and motivation in the university agenda in several ways, in order to make the most of the human capital generated to transform it in economic and social utility.

Litzenberg, K. K. (2010) reported that some characteristics about the students, they have experiencing a difficult career selection process since their parents are expecting them to select a career path and they are prone to procrastination.

Li *et al.*(2011) stated that with the emergence of diversified horticultural and food industries a strong need of Asian students arises for counselling and feedback as they attempt to construct and follow their personal career paths. Formal mentoring programmes have been guiding such processes in many countries and across various disciplines and sectors, especially in developed countries.

Stan *et al.*(2012) reported that students of agricultural universities need a good grasp of English in order to communicate a set of professional skills and to perform job-related functions both at home and abroad. English for specific purpose should be taught as a subject matter important to the students, integrated in their real world.

Gatto*et al.*(2012) suggested that a cooking, nutrition and gardening after-college program in a garden-based setting can improve attitudes and preferences for fruits and vegetables in Latino youth, which may lead to improved nutritional habits and dietary intake and reduced health disparities.

Rai (2016) in her study entitled factors affecting academic performance and aspirations of undergraduate students of Punjab Agricultural University, Ludhiana, revealed that about 15.00 per cent students aspired for government job and private job, respectively.

Chapter-III

RESEARCH METHODOLOGY

The main purpose of this chapter is to deal with various methods and procedure used with respect to selection of areas and locale of the study, sampling designs, data collection procedures, variables under study, their empirical measurements and statistical methods employed for the analysis of the data. This chapter has been discussed under various heads as follows:

3.1 Locale of the study.

3.2 Sampling design and selection of the respondents.

3.3 Selection of variables and empirical measurements.

3.4 Data collection procedures.

3.5 Statistical methods used.

3.1 Locale of the study

In Utter Pradesh, there are 04 agricultural universities but two main and old state agricultural universities namely C.S.A.U.A. & T. Kanpur; A.N.D.U.A. & T. Ayodhya.

Table 3.1.1: Information about the district (Census-2011):

Sr.no.	Particulars	Figures	
		Kanpur Nagar	Ayodhya
1.	Bus stops	324	68
2.	Railway stations	21	22

RESEARCH METHODOLOGY

3.	Total population	4,5729541	2,468,371
a.	Rural population	1,621,654	2,125,588
b.	Urban population	173,438	342,783
c.	Male	2,469,114	1,258,455
d.	Female	2,103,837	1,209,916
4.	Total literacy percentage	77.6	70.63
a.	Male literacy percentage	79.38	80.21
b.	Female literacy percentage	63.03	60.72
5.	Length of canal (km)	822	1225
6.	Government tube wells	353	851
7.	Personal tube wells and pump set	59160	78106
8.	Veterinary hospital	23	35
9.	Artificial Insemination centre	56	76
10.	Primary health centre	32	12
11.	Degree colleges	25	15
12.	Universities	2	2
13.	Total geographical area (sq. km.)	3,156	2,342

Source: Census-2011

Selection of the university and college:

The study was purposively confined to state agricultural universities, C. S. A. U.A. &T. Kanpur, and A.N.U.A. & T. Kumarganj, Ayodhya. These universities have at present time different colleges (College of Agriculture, College of Horticulture& Forestry, College of Fisheries, College of Veterinary Science & Animal Husbandry, College of Home

RESEARCH METHODOLOGY

Science, College of Agriculture Engineering & Technology, College of Biotechnology, College of Agri-Business Management) one of which, college of Agriculture was selected purposively.

Table- 3.1.2.: Location and situation of other institution

Sr.No.	Place	Distance from (Km)	
		A.N.D.U.A.T.Ayodhya.	C.S.A.U.A.T. Kanpur.
1.	District Head Quarter	42	08
2.	Block Head Quarter	11	05
3.	Bus stop	03	1.5
4.	Weekly Market Centre	03	1.5
5.	Cooperative societies	01	05
6.	Primary School	04	0.5
7.	College	02	1.5
8.	Railway Station	42	1.5
9.	Hospital	02	0.5
10.	Post Office	01	0.5

3.2: Sampling design and selection of the respondents:

There are 260 total students who are studying in 1st and 2nd year of M.Sc. (Ag) program under different disciplines of two selected universities. These students went classified into three caste i.e.; SC & ST,

RESEARCH METHODOLOGY

OBC and General. A total 120 studentswent selected randomlyas respondents by using proportionate random sampling technique.

An interview scheduled was prepared keeping in view the objectives and variables to be studied. The personal interview method was employed for data collection from the respondents of the two selected universities.

Table-3.1: Total selected respondents from the sample college.

Uni./Category / Class		A.N.D.U.A&T. Ayodhya				C.S.A.U.A&T. Kanpur				All Total
		UR	OBC	SC/ST	Total	UR	OBC	SC/ST	Total	
M.Sc. (Ag.) 1st & 2nd	P	60	40	40	140	40	40	40	120	260
	S	20	20	20	60	20	20	20	60	120

P= Population, S=Sample

3.3 Selection of variables and their empirical measurements

Table-3.3 Variables to be studied:

S. No.	Variables	Measurements
A.	Independent variables:	
1.	Age	Chronological age class developed.
2.	Education	Trivedi and Pareek (1964) with suitable modifications
3.	Caste	As per government norms
4.	Extracurricular activities	Index developed
5.	Family type	Trivedi and Pareek (1964) with suitable modifications
6.	Size of family	-do-

RESEARCH METHODOLOGY

7.	Family income	-do-
8.	Family occupation	Schedule developed
9.	Housing pattern	-do-
10.	Family land holding	Government of India category (1991)
11.	OGPA	Actual
12.	Communication media possession	Schedule developed
13.	Utilization pattern of ICT tools	Schedule developed.
14.	Economic motivation	Scale developed by Supe (1969) with some modifications.
15.	Achievement motivation	-do-
B.	**Dependent variables**:	
1.	Consciousness for career opportunities	Index developed
2.	Motivational sources	-do-
3.	Career preference	
C.	Constraints regarding conscious job opportunities and preferences.	Open ended responses
D.	Suggestions to overcome the constraints	Open ended responses

RESEARCH METHODOLOGY

A. Independent Variables:

Age:

Age of the students was worked out on the basis of actual age of the respondents, the age categories were made according to mean and standard deviation duly computed for the purpose.

Education:

Education of the respondent was judged from the level of formal education achieved and number of years spent in by the respondents.

Caste:

Caste of the respondents was categorized into three subcategories as per government norms viz.

(a) **General caste:** This category includes Brahmin, Thakur and Kayastha.

(b) **Backward caste:** This category includes Ahir, Chaursiya, Maurya, Kurmi, Kohar, Barbar, Fakir and Lohar.

(c) **Scheduled castes:** This category is concerned with Washeman, Chamar and pasi.

the scores were assigned to various caste categories as general caste (0), Backword caste (1) and scheduled caste/ scheduled tribes (2).

Marital status:

The scores were assigned to two marital statuses like (a)married and(b)unmarried.

Familial variables:

3.3.4 Family Type:

RESEARCH METHODOLOGY

It was worked out on two types (a) single and (b) joint. The scores assigned to family types were 0 and 1 for single and joint family, respectively.

3.3.5 Family Size:

For family size, the scores 1, 2, and 3 were assigned to three categories viz., small (up to 4 members), medium (5 to 13) and large (14 to above) respectively and it were formed on the basis of mean S.D., mean +. S.D. and mean + S.D.

Family occupation:

The occupation of the families was worked out on the basis of enterprises which contribute more than 50 pec cent shares in the total income was considered as main and below then that subsidiary. Occupation of the families it was categorized into following categories:

(1) Agricultural salespersons (0)
(2) Caste- based occupation (1)
(3) Service (2)
(4) Agriculture (3)
(5) Business (4)
(6) Dairying (5)
(7) Government jobs(6)

Family income:

Family income of the respondents was calculated in money value with a unit of rupees considering all concerned sources. Income categories of annual family were framed on the basis of minimum 180000 and maximum 450000 with suitable class intervals.

RESEARCH METHODOLOGY

(1) Up to 100,000; (1,00,0001 to 2,00,000; (3) 2,00,001 to 3,00,000; (4) 3,00,001 to 4,00,000; (5) 4,00,001 and above.

Housing pattern:

To find out the housing pattern of the respondents, four type of houses were categorized viz.,

(a) Hut (b) Kuchha (c) Pucca and (d) Mixed houses were 0, 1, 2, 3, respectively.

Land holding:

Size of land holding was grouped into five categories viz., (i) Landless, (ii) Marginal (below 2.5 acre) (iii) Small (2.5 to acre) (iv) Medium (5 to 7.5) and (v) Large (7.5 acre and above).

Economic motivation:

The scale developed by Supe (1969) was used to measure the economic motivation with a little modification. There were six statements in the economic motivation, bearing five points continuumviz., strongly agree, agree, undecided, disagree and strongly disagree. The score assigned to the points were 5,4,3, 2, and 1 respectively against the positive statements and reverse for negative statements. Respondents were grouped into three categories based on (i) mean- SD(low), (ii) mean +. SD (medium) and (iii) mean + SD (high), respectively.

Achievement motivation:

Achievement motivation has six statements, bearing five points continuum viz., strongly agree, agree, undecided, disagree and strongly disagree. The score assigned to the points were 5,4,3, 2, and 1 respectively against the positive statements and reverse for negative statements.

RESEARCH METHODOLOGY

Respondents were grouped into three categories based on (i) mean- SD (low), (ii) mean +. SD (medium) and (iii) mean + SD (high), respectively.

Communication media use pattern:

To the communication media use patten, the availability and contact pattern were included. So, for as the contact of the respondents with each communication source is concerned, each source was measured on six points continuum (none, very few, few, much, very much and very-2 much)and 1, 2, 3, 4, 5 and 6, scores were assigned to them respectively. A rank order was placed to them for interpretation.

Communication technology use:

The communication technology use pattern was measured on the basis of hours like as how much time do you devote to using communication technology in a day for career plan?............ hours respectively.

Usefulness of communication technology in career preference:

The various usefulness of communication technologies in career preference like; mobile phone, television, internet service, continuum, radio, multimedia respectively. Each source was measured on three points; not useful (1), useful (2) and very useful (3) respectively.

Purpose in use of communication technology:

To study the purpose in use of communication technologies, the availability of communication technologies was included. So far as the contact of the respondents with communication technologies is concerned, each purpose was measured on 3 points continuum (never, sometimes and mostly) and 1, 2,& 3 scores were assigned to them respectively.

RESEARCH METHODOLOGY

A. DEPENDENT VARIABLES:

1. Consciousness about career opportunities:

The scores were assigned to various awareness about career opportunities criteria like; 1.... N

2. Motivational sources:

The various motivational area like; love motivates, knowledge motivates, compassion motivates and economic motivates. Each source was measured on 3 points continuum least preferred (1), more preferred (2) most preferred and (3) least preferred scores were assigned to them respectively. A work order was placed to them for interpretation.

3. Career preferences:

The scores were assigned to various career preferences criteria like; Agriculture Field Officers, Civil services/ Admirative jobs, Educational and research institute jobs, Argo-based public jobs, private based private sector jobs, General jobs, Farming, Self- employment respectively.

C. Constraints analysis

To analyse the constraints relating to career preference of agricultural students a list of all possible problems under categories *viz.,* personal, financial, government and social level. The seriousness of every constraint was measured on the basis of open indent responses of correspondence.

Suggestion measures:

suggestionto overcome the constraints relating to consciousness jobs opportunities and career preferenceswere asked from the students. The

RESEARCH METHODOLOGY

frequency distribution was done and percentage calculated for description.

3.4: Data collection procedures:

A structured schedule for data collection was designed and exercised by interviewing with few respondents for pre-testing. Then, the suitable modifications were made according to need of this study. Thereafter, the data were collected from the respondents through personal interview method.

3.5 Statistical methods used;

The percentage, average and S.D. were used for making simple interpretation.

1. Percentage (%)

The frequency of a particular cell was divided by total number of respondents in the particular category and multiplied by 100 for calculating percentage.

I. Average ($\bar{X}$)

The average (x) was calculated by adding the total scores obtained by the respondents and divided it by the total number of respondents using the following formula.

$$(\bar{X}) = \Sigma\, x/n$$

Where,

$\bar{X}$ = Average or mean

Σx = sum of all the scores obtained by respondents

n = total number of respondents in the sample.

RESEARCH METHODOLOGY

(iii) Standard deviation (σ):

S.D. is the square root of mean of the squares of all deviations, the directions being measured from the arithmetic mean of the distribution. It is commonly developed by symbol sigma (σ)

$$S.D. (\sigma) = \sum d^2 / n$$

Where,

Σ = Standard deviation
d = Deviation of variables mean
n = Total number of items

Chapter-IV

RESULTS AND DISCUSION

The findings and inference drawn in respect to the specific objectives of the study on the basis of analysis by using relevant statistical techniques have been presented in this chapter.

The finding of this study has been divided and discussed into following sub heads:

5.1 Profile of the respondents.

5.2 Consciousness of about career opportunities among the respondents.

5.3 Motivational sources of respondents about career preferences.

5.4 Career preferences of the respondents.

5.5 Constraints

5.6 Suggestion measures.

5.1 Profile of the respondents:

Age of respondents

Table- 5.1.1: Distribution of respondents according to age:

N=120

Sr. No.	Age categories	Respondents	
		No	(%)
1.	20 to 22 years	28	23.33

2.	23 to 24 years	74	61.66
3.	25 to 26 years	18	15.00
	Total	120	100.00

Mean= 22.73, SD= 1.25, Min. = 21-year, Max. = 25-year

The Table 5.1.1 that maximum number of the respondents (61.66) were observed in the category of 23 to 24 years of respectively. so, it focuses that the agriculture PG students of 23 to 24 years of age category were observed to be more.

Education level of respondents:

Table- 5.1.2: Distribution of respondents according to their educational level:

N=120

Sr. No.	Categories	Respondents	
		No.	(%)
1.	M.Sc. (Ag.) I year	48	40
2.	M.Sc. (Ag.) II year	72	60
	Total	120	100.00

The Table 5.1.2 reveals that the ratio between M.Sc. (Ag) first year and second year students was formed to be 2: 3.

Caste Categories:

Table-5.1.3: Distribution of respondents according to caste:

N=120

Sr. No.	Categories	Respondents	
		No.	(%)
1.	General caste	42	35
2.	Other Backward Caste	58	48.33
3.	Scheduled caste/Scheduled Tribes	20	16.66
	Total	**120**	**100.00**

The Table 5.1.3 indicates the (16%) students belonged to SC/ST caste, (35%) General Caste and 48.33% respondents comes under Other Backward Caste (OBC) respectively. thus, it can be concluded that OBC caste had dominancy so for as agriculture study is concerned.

Marital status:

5.1.4: Distribution of respondents according to marital status:

N=120

Sr. No.	Categories	Respondents	
		No	(%)
1.	Married	26	21.66
2.	Unmarried	94	78.33
	Total	**120**	**100.00**

It is obvious from the Table 5.1.4 that maximum number of the respondents was observed unmarried (78.33) against married respondents (21.66) respectively.

Family type:

Table- 5.1.5: Distribution of respondents according to family type.

N = 120

Sr. No.	Categories	Respondents	
		No.	(%)
1.	Single/ Nuclear	46	38.33
2.	Joint	74	61.67
	Total	120	100.00

The Table 5.1.5 indicates that 61.67 percent respondents were residing in joint family system and remaining 38.33 percent respondents were observed in nuclear family. It shows that joint family system was dominant among the families of agriculture.

Family size:

RESULTS AND DISCUSION

Table- 5.1.6: Distribution of respondents according to family size.

N=120

Sr. No.	Categories	Respondents	
		No.	(%)
1.	Small (up to 4 members)	38	31.67
2.	Medium (5 to 10 members)	55	45.83
3.	Large (11 and above)	27	22.50
	Total	120	100.00

The Table- 5.1.6 that 45.83 percent of the respondent's families were observed such who had up to 4 members followed by 31.67 percent respondents' families having 5 to 10 members and only 22.50 percent respondents' families were found having 11 and above family members in their families. The range between minimum and maximum number of family members was recorded from 2 to 15.

Family Occupation: -

Table- 5.1.7: Distribution of respondents according to family occupation.

N=120

Sr. No.	Category	Respondents		Rank
		Number	Percentage	
1.	Private jobs	15	12.50	IV
2.	Caste based	25	20.83	I

	occupation			
3.	Service	10	8.33	VII
4.	Agriculture	20	16.67	II
5.	Business	8	6.67	VIII
6.	Dairying	12	10.00	VI
7.	Government jobs	16	13.33	III
8	Agricultural salespersons	14	11.67	V
	Total	**120**	**100**	

There are eight categories of occupation and Table 5.1.7 indicated that the highest number of respondents are doing caste-based occupation (20.83%) followed by agriculture (16.67%), government jobs (13.33%), private jobs (12.50%), agricultural salespersons (11.67%), dairying (10.00%), service (8.33%) and business (6.67%) respectively.

Family income:

Table- 5.1.8: Distribution of respondents according to family income (Rs.)

N= 120

Sr. No.	Income categories	Respondents (No.)	Percentages
1.	Up to 100000	25	20.83
2.	100001 to 200000	35	29.16
3.	200001 to 300000	40	33.33

4.	300001 to 400000	15	12.50
5.	400001 and above	5	4.17
	Total	120	100.00

Average = 262008, min.=100000, max.= 450000

It is clearly from Table 5.1.8 that maximum (33.33%) of the respondents were form those families whose annual income were found in the categories of Rs. 200001to 300000 followed by other categories *viz.,* 29.16% (100001 to 200000), 20.83% (up to 100000), 12.50% (300001 to 4000000 and 4.17% (400001 to above) respectively.

Housing pattern:

Table- 5.1.9: Distribution of respondents according to housing pattern.

N=120

Sr. No.	categories	Respondents (No.)	Percentages
1.	Hut	0	0
2.	Kuchha	15	12.50
3.	Pucca	82	68.33
4.	Mixed	23	19.17
	Total	120	100.00

The Table 5.1.9 pertaining to the type of houses possession that 68.33 percent respondents were having pucca houses followed by

19.17% (mixed) and 12.50% (kuchha) respectively. Therefore, pucca housing pattern is more than other housing pattern.

Land holding:

Table- 5.1.10: Distribution of respondents according to land housing.

N = 120

Sr. No.	categories	Respondents (No.)	Percentages
1.	Landless	12	10.00
2.	Marginal (below 2.5 acre)	36	30.00
3.	Small (2.5 acre to 5 acre)	28	23.33
4.	Medium (5 acres to 7.5 acre)	25	20.83
5.	Large (7.5 and above)	19	15.83
	Total	120	100.00

Mean = 2.73, Min. = 0, Max. = 17 acre

It is clearly from Table 5.1.10 indicates that maximum respondents (30.00%) were found in the land holding categories of marginal farmers (below 2.5 acre) followed by 23.33% small farmers (2.5 acre to 5 acre), 20.83 % medium farmer (5 acre to 7.5 acre), 15.83% large famers (7.5 acre and above) and 10.00% respondents was found landless farmers categories respectively.

Communication media possession:

Table- 5.1.11: Distribution of respondents according to communication media possession

Sr. No.	Categories	At family level	percent	At personal level	Percent
1.	News paper	85	70.83	80	66.67
2.	Radio	40	33.00	65	54.16
3.	Television	80	66.67	45	37.50
4.	Computer	20	16.60	80	66.67
5.	Magazine	00	00	90	75.00
6.	Book	25	20.83	95	79.16
7.	Journal	00	00	80	66.67
8.	Telephone	00	00	00	00
9.	Cellular phone	120	100.00	120	120.00
10.	Periodicals	00	00	75	62.50

The Table 5.1.11 shows that a majority of respondents (83.33% and 85.00%) at personal level and family level was observed possessing cellular phone with them. The remaining respondents who had other communication media in descending order at family level *viz.*, radio (33.00%), newspaper (70.83%), television (66.67%), magazine (00%), book (20.83%), computer (16.60%), journal (00%), telephone (00%), periodicals (00%) respectively.

At personal level the person who had other communication media with them were in descending order *viz.,* book (79.16%), magazine, (75.00%), newspaper, computer, journal (66.67%), periodical (62.50%), radio (54.16), television (37.50%) and telephone (00%), respectively. Therefore, it may be concluded that the respondents as well as families have a good (average percent at family level is 52.08% and at personal level 61.64%) number of communication media possession.

Economic motivation:

Table- 5.1.12: Distribution of respondents according to degree of agreement/ disagreement statement of economic motivation.

S.No.	Statements	SA (5)	A (4)	UD (3)	DA (2)	SDA (1)
1.	A agriculture student should work to have higher education for economic profits.	39	30	34	16	14
2.	The most successful agriculture students in one who makes most profits.	53	25	32	18	11
3.	A agriculture student should try any new idea of educational side which may earn	28	34	28	26	6

		SA	A	UD	DA	SDA
	his/her more money.					
4.	It is a dificult for agriculture student to make good start in education or entrepreneurship unless being assisted finacially.	36	22	18	20	24
5.	A agriculture student must earn his/her living but the most important thing is that the life cannot be defiend in economic terms.	22	16	34	18	30
6.	A agriculture student should have other types of education to increase monitory status stauts in comparision to only agriculture.	30	28	22	17	23
Average percentage		25.13	21.67	16.20	19.00	18.00

SA= Strongly Agree, A= Agree, UD= Un Decided, DA= Disagree, SDA= Strongly Disagree

It is evident from the Table- 5.1.12 that maximum number of respondents (25.13%) were found having strongly agree of economic motivation, followed by agried (21.67%), disagree (19.00%),strongly disagrre (18.00%) and undecieded (16.20%) respondents respectively.

Table- 5.1.13: Category wise distribution of respondents according to economic motivation

N=120

Sr. No.	Categories	Respondents	
		No.	(%)
1.	Low (up to 18)	55	55.83
2.	Medium (19 to 22)	42	35
3.	High (23 and above)	23	19.16
	Total	120	100.00

Mean =17.55, SD= 2.11, Min.=14, Max.= 24

It is obvious from Table 5.1.13 that maximum number of respondents (55.83%) was found having low category (up to 18) of economic motivation followed by (35.00%) medium and (19.16%) high category respectively.

Achievement motivation: -

Table- 5.1.14:Distribution of respondents according to degree of agreement/disagreement statement of Achievement motivation.

Sr. No.	Statements	SA	A	UD	DA	SDA
1.	Work should come first even if one can get proper rest in order to achievement one's goals.	34	30	20	16	20
2.	It is little to be intent with whatever better one has than to be always struggling for more.	26	34	18	22	20
3.	No matter what I have done? I always want to do more.	20	22	34	18	26
4.	I would like to try has at something really difficult even it proves than. I cannot do it.	20	16	30	34	20
5.	The way things are now a day's discourse one to work hard.	28	22	30	20	20
6.	One should succeed in occupation even if one has to neglect his family.	20	36	22	32	10
	Average percentage	**25.8**	**20.00**	**18.40**	**16.20**	**19.61**

= Strongly Agree, A= Agree, UD= Un Decided, DA= Disagree, SDA= Suddenly Disagrreed

Table- 5.1.15: Distribution of respondents according to achievement motivation

N=120

Sr. No.	Categories	Respondents	
		No.	(%)
1.	Low (up to 18)	35	29.16
2.	Medium (19 to 22)	45	37.50
3.	High (23 and above)	40	33.33
	Total	120	100.00

Mean =20.88, SD= 2.32, Min.=16, Max.= 26

It is obvious from Table 5.1.14 that maximum number of respondents (37.50%) was found having low category (up to 18) of economic motivation followed by (29.16%) medium and (33.33%) high category respectively.

5.2 Consciousness about career opportunities:

Table- 5.2.1: Distribution of respondents according to degree of consciousness about career opportunities.

N= 120

Sr. No.	Career opportunities and consciousness	Respondents	Percentage	Rank
1.	PCS	46	38.33	I

2.	IFS	38	31.67	II
3.	SSC	35	29.16	III
4.	AAO	33	27.5	IV
5.	Agriculture Officer	25	20.83	V
6.	Banking	24	20.00	VI
7.	Professor	22	18.33	VII
8.	BDO	20	16.67	VIII
9.	CDS	19	15.83	IX
10.	VDO	18	15	X
11.	SMS	15	12.5	XI
12.	Extension Worker	12	10	XII
13.	Teaching	11	9.16	XIII
14.	ARS	10	8.33	XVI
15.	ABM	8	6.67	XV
16.	Private	7	5.83	XVI

The Table 5.2.1 the degree of consciousness about career opportunities as indicated by the respondents. It is clear from above data that the PCS job 38.33% was highly conscious by the respondents remaining students/respondents who had other consciousness about career opportunities with them were in descending order viz., IFS (31.67%), SSC (29.16%), AAO(27.50%), Agriculture Officer (20.83%), Banking (20.00%), Professor (18.33%), BDO (16.67%), CDS (15.83%), VDO (15.00%), SMS (12.50%), Extension Officer (10.00%), Teaching (9.16%), ARS (8.33%), and ABM (6.67%) and private (5.83%) respectively. Therefore, the PCS, IFS and Banking jobs were most awarded jobs with the respondents.

5.3 Motivational sources for career preference:

Table- 5.3.1: Distribution of respondents according to love motivating sources.

Sr. No.	Sources	Degree of motivation			Total	Mean score value	Rank
		Most P. (3)	More P. (2)	Least P. (1)			
1.	Father	70	30	20	290	2.41	I
2.	Mother	60	25	15	245	2.04	II
3.	Brother	22	20	25	121	1.00	IX
4.	Sister	50	25	35	235	1.95	III
5.	Friends	36	25	10	168	1.4	VI
6.	Relatives	29	30	8	155	1.29	VII
7.	Seniors	25	22	15	134	1.11	VIII
8.	Teachers	40	30	30	200	1.67	IV
9.	Ideal person	45	20	10	185	1.54	V
10.	Leader	22	15	40	116	9.67	X
11.	Business person	16	18	20	104	0.87	XI
12.	Purohit/Guru	13	7	26	79	0.65	XIV
13.	Self	15	21	13	100	0.83	XII

The Table 5.3.1 show that maximum motivating source was summarized as father ranked at with mean scores 2.41 followed by mother (2.04) ranked II, sister (1.95) ranked III, teacher (1.67) ranked VI, ideal person (1.54) ranked V, friends (1.4) ranked VI, relatives (1.29) ranked VII, seniors (1.11) ranked VIII, brother (1.00) ranked IX, Leader (9.67) ranked X, business person (0.87) respectively. So, the father, mother and sister were most important motivating respondents.

Table- 5.3.2: Distribution of respondents according to Knowledge motivating sources.

Sr. No.	Sources	Degree of motivation			Total	Mean score value	Rank
		Most P. (3)	More P. (2)	Least P. (1)			
1.	Father	80	30	25	325	2.70	I
2.	Mother	73	28	30	305	2.54	II
3.	Brother	60	25	11	241	2.01	VIII
4.	Sister	55	20	35	240	2.00	IX
5.	Friends	62	24	30	264	2.20	IV
6.	Relatives	50	27	29	233	1.94	X
7.	Seniors	65	20	14	249	2.07	V
8.	Teachers	59	35	34	281	2.34	III
9.	Ideal person	49	25	24	221	1.84	XIII
10.	Leader	45	20	20	195	1.62	XIV

RESULTS AND DISCUSION

11.	Business person	40	18	17	173	1.44	XV
13.	Self	61	35	34	287	2.03	VII
14.	TV	35	25	14	169	1.40	XVI
15.	News paper	46	35	37	245	2.04	VI
16.	Magazines	34	18	16	154	1.28	XVII
17.	Internet	26	25	19	147	1.22	XVIII
18.	Seminars	47	28	30	227	1.89	XI

The Table 5.3.2 that show the knowledge motivates sources father ranked at first with the mean value score of 2.70 followed by mother (2.54) ranked II, teacher (2.34) ranked III, friend (2.20) ranked IV, seniors (2.07) ranked V, newspaper (2.04) ranked VI, self (2.03) ranked VII, brother (2.01) VIII, sister (2.00) ranked IX, relative (1.94) ranked X, seminar 1.89 ranked XI, purohit/guru (1.88) ranked XII, ideal person (1.84) ranked XIII, leader (1.62) ranked XIV, business person (1.44) ranked XV, TV (1.40) ranked XVI, magazine (1.28) ranked XVII and internet 1.22 ranked XVIII respectively. Hence the father, mother and teacher is the more important for knowledge motivational source for respondents.

Table- 5.3.3: Distribution of respondents according toCompassion motivating sources.

Sr. No.	Sources	Degree of motivation			Total	Mean score value	Rank
		Most	More	Least			

RESULTS AND DISCUSION

		P. (3)	P. (2)	P. (1)			
1.	Father	68	32	40	308	2.56	I
2.	Mother	41	30	40	223	1.85	II
3.	Brother	27	40	27	188	1.56	III
4.	Sister	42	17	06	166	1.38	V
5.	Friends	45	20	08	183	1.52	IV
6.	Relatives	33	15	21	144	1.20	VIII
7.	Seniors	37	17	02	147	1.22	VII
8.	Teachers	36	25	08	166	1.37	VI
9.	Ideal person	24	24	16	112	0.93	X
10.	Leader	27	08	11	108	0.90	XI
11.	Business person	08	35	09	103	0.85	XII
12.	Purohit/Guru	16	15	13	91	0.75	XIII
13.	Self	33	10	11	130	1.08	IX
14.	TV	16	15	11	89	0.74	XIV
15.	News paper	6	23	16	80	0.67	XV
16.	Magazines	15	14	09	82	0.68	XVI
17.	Internet	26	06	08	98	0.81	XVII
18.	Seminars	12	12	14	74	0.61	XVIII

The Table 5.3.3 show that the father followed by mother, brother, friend's and sisterwith mean score value 2.56, 1.85, 1.56, 1.52 and 1.38 respectively were found to be most important compassion motivational source among all. And the other compassion motivational sources is also important to agriculture students.

Table- 5.3.4: Distribution of respondents according to Economic motivating sources.

Sr. No.	Sources	Degree of motivation			Total	Mean score value	Rank
		Most P. (3)	More P. (2)	Least P. (1)			
1.	Father	68	25	16	245	2.04	I
2.	Mother	55	25	24	239	1.99	II
3.	Brother	49	17	32	213	1.77	III
4.	Sister	35	20	16	161	1.34	VI
5.	Friends	46	18	07	181	1.50	IV
6.	Relatives	24	18	13	121	1.00	XI
7.	Seniors	29	17	19	140	1.16	VII
8.	Teachers	45	18	07	178	1.48	V
9.	Ideal person	17	38	10	137	1.14	VIII
10.	Leader	36	10	08	136	1.13	IX
11.	Business person	33	08	18	133	1.10	X
12.	Purohit/Guru	22	12	04	98	0.81	XIV
13.	Self	21	09	11	92	0.76	XV

14.	TV	14	08	16	74	0.61	XVII
15.	News paper	23	17	07	110	0.91	XII
16.	Magazines	22	2	11	81	0.67	XVI
17.	Internet	26	12	07	109	0.90	XIII
18.	Seminars	12	02	04	44	0.36	XVIII

It is obvious from Table 5.3.4 indicated the father followed by mother, brother, friends, and relatives mean score value is 2.04, 1.99, 1.77, 1.50 and 1.00 respectively were found to be most important sources to economic motivates for agriculture students. And all other sources are also half full to economic motivates for respondents.

5.4 Career preferences:

Table- 5.4.1: Distribution of respondents according to career preferences:

Sr. No.	Career preferences	Respondents		ranks
		No.	present	
A.	Government jobs			
1.	A F O	85	70.83	II
2.	Civil services or administrative jobs	95	79.16	I
3.	State Government jobs	46	38.33	VI
4.	Research and teaching	57	47.50	V
5.	Agricultural operation manager	40	33.33	VIII
6.	Agricultural scientist	80	66.67	III

B.	Non- government jobs			
1.	General jobs	70	58.33	IV
2.	Farm manager	45	37.50	VII
3.	Self- employment	35	29.16	IX
4.	Campus placement	32	26.67	X

The Table- 5.4.1 shows the degree of career preferences as preferred by the respondents. It is the clear from the above data that the Civil services jobs are mostly respondents' preferences and ranking at – I. Followed by other government and non- government jobs respectively.

5.5 Constraints:

Constraints in conscious job opportunities and following preferences:

Table 5.5.1 Degree of seriousness of constraints.

Sr. No.	Constraints	No.	Percentage	Rank
1.	Lack of command on my own desires	110	91.67	IV
2.	Personal responsibility	85	70.83	VIII
3.	Fear of failure	74	61.67	XI
4.	Lack of time for thinking about conscious jobs.	115	95.83	II
5.	Heavy work load in college	70	58.33	XII
6.	Heavy work load in home	80	66.67	IX

7.	Quality of education	116	96.67	I
8.	No pre exam training for governmental jobs.	105	87.50	V
9.	It is hard to get a government job.	95	79.16	VII
10.	Lack of motivation in education system.	112	93.33	III
11.	Lack of knowledge about agricultural jobs.	75	62.50	X

The Table 5.5.1 envisage the rank order of personal constraints *viz.,* low quality of education at I (96.67%) followed by Lack of time for thinking about conscious jobs. (95.83%), lack of motivation in education system (93.33%), lack of command on my own desires (91.67%), no pre exam training for governmental jobs (87.50%), lack of time for thinking about conscious jobs (80.00%), it is hard to get to a governmental jobs (79.16%), personal responsibility (70.83%), heavy work load in home (66.67%), lack of knowledge about agricultural jobs (62.50%), fear of failure (61.67%) and heavy work load in college (58.33%) respondents respectively.

5.6 Suggestion measures:

Table-5.6: Suggestion measures to overcome the constraints in career preference of agriculture students.

Sr. No.	Suggestion measures	No.	Percentages	Rank
1.	Knowledge about agriculture jobs must be provided for	87	72.50	VI

		students to increase the level of preferences.			
2.		Student should develop the feeling responsibility for their career by removing hesitation.	78	65.00	VIII
3.		Knowledge system should be made strong about different preferences available in the area of agriculture.	69	57.50	X
4.		Personality improvement extra classes should be organized for increasing the confidence level of students, so that they could prepare themselves for preferring a job.	110	91.67	III
5.		Students must develop a positive attitude which would increase their interest to know more about the career preferences.	70	58.33	IX

6.	Social norms and values should be turned towards doing the career by the girls. Parents should consider the value of higher education to the girls for improving decision making power among girls.	85	70.83	VII
7.	Fear for disappear by the parents.	65	54.16	XI
8.	Facility for proper counselling about career preferring should be provided for students.	90	75.00	V
9.	Congenial environment should be made by the government to the working girls/women, so that they can refer freely.	92	76.67	IV
10.	Government should have improvement quality of education.	112	93.33	II
11.	Students should have good skills and doing hard work for achievement his/ her goals.	115	95.83	I

RESULTS AND DISCUSION

The Table 5.6.1 indicates that different suggestive measures were perceived by respondents. The suggest ivies such as Students should have good skills and doing hard work for achievement his/her goals ranked at I indicated by 95.83 per cent respondents followed by government should have improvement quality of education (93.33%), Personality improvement extra classes should be organized for increasing the confidence level of students, so that they could prepare themselves for preferring a job(91.67%), Congenial environment should be made by the government to the working girls/women, so that they can refer freely(76.67%), Facility for proper counselling about career preferring should be provided for students(75.00%),Knowledge about agriculture jobs must be provided for students to increase the level of preferences (72.50%), Social norms and values should be turned towards doing the career by the girls. Parents should consider the value of higher education to the girls for improving decision making power among girls (70.83%), Student should develop the feeling responsibility for their career by removing hesitation (65.00%), Students must develop a positive attitude which would increase their interest to know more about the career preferences(58.67%), Knowledge system should be made strong about different preferences available in the area of agriculture (57.50%) and fear for disappear by the parents (54.16%) respondents respectively. Hence, the suggestion mentioned at I, II, and III range were the most considerable suggestions.

Chapter-V

CONCEPTUAL REAME WORK

This chapter deals with the conceptual frame work of various concept covered in this manuscript are as follows:

(1) **Acre:** It is a measuring unit of land of an area of 3.560 Sq. ft or 0.405 ha.

(2) **Age:** it is referring to the chronological age of the respondents in year at the time of interview.

(3) **Awareness:** Awareness is the state or ability to perceive understanding.

(4) **Bibliography:** List of references cited in the chapter of bibliography which has been consulted for writing the manuscript of this dissertation.

(5) **Career:** An occupation undertaken for a significant period of a person's life and with opportunities for progress.

(6) **Caste:** Caste is the permanent type of social stratification of the society into higher and lower categories. It focuses the caste of students belong to.

(7) **Category:** A class, group or type based on same traits, such categories have been framed to categories and interpret according to variables under study.

(8) **Communication media possession:** These are the means by which information or knowledge is passed from one group or individual to another.

(9) **Constraints:** Constraints are problems of hurdles faced by the respondents in playing their roles and function. These were social, economic, technical, personal and marketing etc.

(10) **Data:** Data are defined as facts, figures, etc. known or available information. The primary data were collected from the respondents under study and secondary data from secondary sources for the study.

(11) **Decision pattern:** Decision pattern we believe that understanding towards achievements of the maximum economic yield for maximization of profits of their job preference.

(12) **Education:** It refers to the level of formal education obtained by the respondents.

(13) **Family size:** It refers to the total number of persons living in a family.

(14) **Housing pattern:** It refers to the habitation of the respondents. The villagers get constructed and live there in with their family members.

(15) **Information:** Information is difference in matter energy that effect uncertainty in a situation where a choice exists among a set of alternatives.

(16) **Interview:** Interviews are conducted with selected individuals ' respondents. Interviewing a number of different people on some topic shall quickly reveal a wide range of opinions, attitude a strategy.

(17) **Means:** A measure of central tendency, the sum of all sources divided by their number, more popularly known as arithmetic mean.

(18) **Family:** All members of house hold who live together under one roof and one-man guidance.

(19) Family type: It is two type viz. single and joint family. In a single-family father, mother and their unmarried children are considered while in a joint family the members of two and three generation along with relatives and servants together under one roof with common food system in the family of the respondents.

(20) Family income: It is referring to total income in rupees as earned by all members of family from all sources in particular year.

(21) Motivation: The internal state which stimulates a person to carry out certain activities.

(22) Objectives: it is expression of the ends towards which our efforts are directed.

(23) Occupation: It is conceptualized as the sources of livelihood of the respondents as a job or profession.

(24) Opportunities: A set circumstances that makes it possible to do something. A chance for employment of promotion.

(25) Preference: Act if preferring about any object.

(26) Purposive sample: A type of non-probability sample in which the elements to be included in the sample are selected by the researcher on the basis of special characteristics of the respondents.

(27) Random sampling: The process in which all combinations of units of populations have an equal chance of being selected for investigation.

(28) Range: A measure of dispersion, a difference score obtained by subtracting the smallest score from the largest score in distribution.

(29) **Range order:** Listing of the pupils in order or merit.

(30) **Ranking procedures:** Refers to a method used to arrange classes of pupils or list of marks into rank order.

(31) **Reference:** Note in a publication referring the reader to another passage source person who supplies a recommendation for some seeking, employment or an introduction.

(32) **Respondents:** people who have answered the question asked by an interviewer is a social survey.

(33) **Sample:** A part of population consisting of one or more sampling units selected and examined as representative of the whole population.

(34) **Schedule:** Schedule is the name usually applied to a set of questions which are asked and filled in by the investigator in a face to face situation with another person.

(35) **Size of land holding:** It refers to the possession of land in acres/hectares by respondents.

(36) **Socio-economic profile:** It is the profile of socio- economic component that refer to the status of individual, group, society or organization in varying degrees. In present study, it refers to the socio- economic status, the respondents possess.

(37) **Source:** A place, person, or thing from which something comes of can be obtained.

(38) **Standard deviation:** A measure of dispersion which is square root of the sum of squared deviations of each score from the mean divided by the total number of scores.

(39) **Suggestion:** An idea of plan put forward for consideration.

(40) Variables: which, when measured can present more than one numerical value, variables are of two types as follows:

    (i)   **Dependent variables:** The variable whose value is influenced or is to be predicted is called dependent variable.

    (ii)   **Independent variable:** The variable which influenced the value of dependent variable used for predictor is called independent variable.

Chapter-VI

SUMMARY AND CONCLUSION

The present study entitled **"Study on Consciousness about Career Opportunities and Preference of Agriculture Post Graduates Students in Agricultural Universities (U.P.)** "was under taken the year 2018-20.

Out of 04 agriculture universities, 02 agriculture universities viz. ANDUAT, Kumarganj, Ayodhya and CSAUAT, Kanpur were selected purposively for this study. From the lists, a total number of 120 students/ respondents were selected through proportionate random sampling techniques keeping in view their education categories. The investigator himself had collected the data from the respondents with the help of pre-tested interview schedule.

Analysis of data was done with the use of percentage as well as correlation coefficient to see the relationship between different variables and point scale to find out the career preference of students about the agriculture. The available researches have been presented under the following sub heads:

1. Profile of the respondents.
2. Consciousness of the respondents about career opportunities.
3. Motivational sources for career opportunities.
4. Preference of the respondents about career opportunities.
5. Constraints regarding conscious job opportunities and fulfilling preferences and suggestions to overcome the constraints there of.

1. Profile of respondents: -

1. The mostly respondents (61.66%) were found in as age categories of 23 to 24 years.
2. The maximum number of the respondents (48.33%) were belonging to backward caste.
3. The maximum respondents (78.33%) were unmarried will (21.66%) married.
4. The maximum respondents (55.83%) were observed in the low (up to 18) level of economic motivation.
5. The maximum respondents (37.50%) were observed in medium (19 to 22) level of achievement motivation.
6. Joint families (61.67%) were more than nuclear/ single families (38.33%) respondents respectively.
7. Medium (5 to 10 members) maximum respondents (45.83%) were observed in family size followed by small (up to 4 members) 31.67% and large (11 and above) 22.50% respondents respectively.
8. The maximum number of respondents (33.33%) were found in the category those families who annual income is 200001- 300000 followed by 100001 – 200000 (29.16%), up to 100000 (20.83%), 300001- 400000(12.50%) and 400001 and above (4.17%) respondents respectively.
9. The majority (30.00%) of the respondents were found in the land holding category of marginal (below 2.5 acre) followed by 23.33% in the category of small farmers (2.5 acre to 5 acre), 20.83% in the medium farmers (5acres to 7.5 acres), 15.83% in the large farmers (7.5 and above) and 10.00% landless framers respectively.

2. Consciousness about career opportunities: -

The maximum number of respondents were found aware the PCS jobs ranked at first with 38.33% IFS (31.67%), SSC (29.16%), AAO (27.50%) and Banking (20.00) respectively.

3. Motivational sources for career opportunities.

1. The maximum respondents stated love motivate sources father ranked at first with mean score value (2.41) followed by mother (2.04) and sister (1.95) respectively were found to be important motivational sources among all.

2. The maximum respondents stated knowledge motivate sources father at first with mean score value (2.70) followed by mother (2.54), teachers (2.34), friends (2.20), seniors (2.07) and purohit/guru (1.88) respectively were found to be important motivational sources among all.

3. The maximum respondents stated compassion motivate sources father at first with mean score value (2.56) followed by mother (1.86) and brother (1.56) respectively were found to be important motivational sources among all.

4. The maximum respondents stated economic motivate sources father at first with mean score value (2.04) followed by mother (1.99), brother (1.77) and sister (1.34) respectively were found to be important motivational sources among all.

4. Preference of the respondents about career opportunities

1. Civil services or administrative jobs was all most the preferred job at ranked first, as reported for maximum students prefers government jobs as compared to non-government jobs.

5. Constraints: -

All above 12 constraints regarding constraints jobs opportunities and fulfilling preferences of jobs, the constraints viz, low quality of education system at first ranked followed by gender biasness, lack of motivation in education system, Lack of time for thinking about conscious jobs, No pre exam training for governmental jobs, Lack of command on my own desires and Lack of knowledge about agricultural jobs respectively, were found important which need more attention to remove the same.

Suggestion measures to overcome the constraints above conscious job opportunities for fulfilling of agriculture students: -

Out of eleven suggestive measures to overcome the constraints in career preferences of agriculture students, the suggestive measures like Students should have good skills and doing hard work for achievement his/ her goals had got ranked at first followed by government should have improvement quality of education, Personality improvement extra classes should be organized for increasing the confidence level of students, so that they could prepare themselves for preferring a jobs respectively, were of emerged important and these so and so forth.

Suggestions based on inferences:

Most important suggestion being made in view point of the expressed opinion of the respondents, observations of the investigator and the inferences drawn from the study are as follows:

1. Parent/guardians must provide proper support to students for batter career preference about agriculture.
2. Security and transportation facilities must be provided for working girls/ women.
3. The students must be provided good skills and techniques for achievement his/ her goals.
4. To eradicate gender biasness from the society.
5. The personality improvement extra classes must be planned to students for various jobs.
6. Monitoring and evaluation system also started in class room.
7. Provide proper knowledge about agriculture jobs at right time of the students.
8. Parents/guardians must be changing their attitude towards students work from outside homes.
9. Government should be provided economic support for weaker section of the students.

www.ingramcontent.com/pod-product-compliance
Lightning Source LLC
LaVergne TN
LVHW010605070526
838199LV00063BA/5078